The Power of Living in Choice

By

Dr. Gary Cone

The Cone Center
LIVING IN CHOICE

Revised 2024

Printed in the United States of America

Before delving into the work, write your own story.

_____

_____

_____

_____

_____

_____

_____

_____

_____

_____

_____

_____

_____

_____

_____

_____

_____

Table of contents

ENERGY MATRIX CLEARING SYSTEMS

LEVELS OF RESPONSIBILITY

PRO-ACTIVE	RE-ACTIVE
COURAGE Affirming, empowered, feasible constructive, strong, active, positive, engaged, excited, imaginative, possible, feasible	**ANTAGONISM** Hides inadequacy, attached, annoyed, combative, indignant, bothered, counter-active, burdened, opposing
WILLING Intentional, optimistic, enthusiastic, prepared, courageous, adequate, creative, playful, invigorated, answerable, worthwhile, responsible	**PRIDE/INDIFFERENCE** Belligerent, demanding, scornful, pessimistic, immobilized, numb, unfeeling, stagnant, destructive, disconnected, rigid, detrimental
NEUTRAL Trust, satisfied, interested, fascinated, welcomed, needed, essential, tuned in, appreciated	**ANGER/RESENTMENT** Hides behind "You hurt me and that gives me the right to protect myself", confused, incensed, overwrought, wounded, hysterical, wrathful, fuming, furious, abused, unappreciated, rejected, numb, offended, hurt & used.
ACCEPTANCE Harmonious, forgiving, adaptable, worthy, open, amused, approachable, deserving, choosing to, owning	**DESIRE/HOSTILITY** Blaming, "Someone else is responsible for me not getting what I want.", Frustrated picked on, sarcastic, trapped, mean, deprived, withholding, vindictive
REASON Wise, understanding, bold, proud, daring, protected, selfless, thoughtful, motivated, considerate, understanding	**FEAR** Anxious, escape, "Something will be taken away from me." avoids, uncared for, trapped, disappointed, frightened, threatened, overlooked, unacceptable, unwelcome
LOVE Reverent, benign, revelatory, risking, trusting, caring, knowing, pleasurable, secure, respectful, giving, responsible	**GRIEF** Regretful, despondent, tragic, self-blaming, victim, depressed, unacceptable, morose, despondent, melancholy, defeated, deserted
JOY Serenity, whole, exuberant, fullfilled, energetic, complete, unencumbered	**SHAME** "I won't't survive", humiliation, cowardice, betrayed, disgraced, self-blaming, dishonored, bad (embarrassed), doubtful
PEACE Perfection, bliss, harmony, trust, thoughtfulness, nurturing, complete	**SEPARATION/GUILT** Self destructive, non-entity, "God does not love me, therefore, I am unlovable", lost, ruined, condemned, ineffectual, conquered
ENLIGHTENMENT Pure, sincere, ineffable, aware, respectful, appreciating, powerful	**APATHY** Waiting to succumb, resigned, hopeless, takes no responsibility for cause, uncared for, insignificant, powerlessness, distrustful & suspicious

EMOTION — FEELING — THOUGHT (left)
EMOTION — FEELING — THOUGHT (right)

The Cone Center
LIVING IN CHOICE

Chapter 1:
EMCS©
Living in Choice Levels of
Responsibility

EXPLANATION OF THE CHART:
EMCS© LIVING IN CHOICE LEVELS OF RESPONSIBILITY

The Law of Attraction responds to the way a **Reflex/Belief** is put into our thoughts and held in place. It always reflects our intention, negative or positive. I call this a "mirror of life." Sometimes, we think all we can hope for is a small, contained control over our environment. We want to manage our lives and the people in it to such a degree that we experience the least amount of pain possible. Barring that, a modicum of what we call "control" would at least be passable; we can handle that. We project our personal disappointments onto others and call it "blame." When the object of our blame does not respond in the exact way we want, we decide immediately that it is our fault. The resulting thought is, "I am faulty now; I deserve the blame because I am not good enough, not perfect, or just stupid." This response perpetuates the negative pattern. We can quickly come to believe the pattern of self-condemnation we have established for ourselves. We must never listen to it, or we will get stuck in a bad fairy tale we made up about ourselves a long time ago and have put out into the world at large. Guess what? It will come right back to us if we don't surrender it to the higher self. We tend to recreate patterns that cause myriad problems for us. This manifests a belief system that punishes us and results in our feeling we have no way out.

We all experience life according to the core beliefs we hold. What we believe about ourselves is always fundamentally what holds power over us. The world outside is the key. If we are alive, we are happy. No sad or ugly idea we have about ourselves can stop this gorgeous world we are so lucky to live in. That gorgeous world will always help us if we let it.

I created the *EMCS Living In Choice© Chart* as a visual tool to show how negative core beliefs create unhealthy thoughts, feelings, and emotions. The first division on the right side includes three distinct choices a person can make for him/herself: **APATHY, SEPARATION/GUILT, and SHAME.** On the left side appear the positive choices: **Enlightenment, Peace, and Joy.** The right side of the chart maps out the bad reactions one is capable of succumbing to. It is entirely in the REACTIVE realm, as is each person if he/she does not make the positive, self-loving choices that the left side of the chart leads to. Each side of the chart shows a very different world. One world is truth, and the other world is the negative ego lashing out, begging a person to keep harming her/himself. The left side represents love in every manifestation humans are capable of imagining. The right side shows only a deviation from such love. One side has nothing to do with the other.

When we focus wholeheartedly on the PRO-ACTIVE state of mind, the sad and harmful REACTIVE side diminishes in power until it dissipates and utterly dissolves, leaving us unharmed at last. As the saying goes, "No one can serve two masters..."[1] We give our energy to our proactive state of mind, or we let negativity take us away to react as we may to what our ego tricks us into believing. It is impossible to do both at the same time.

Core Negative Beliefs

At the bottom of the *EMCS© Living In Choice© Chart,* the **Reactive, Reflex/Belief** section represents long-held and damaging ideas about ourselves that are largely unavailable to us. We are

---

[1] Luke 16:13. Bible, New Living Translation, 2007

unaware that these beliefs are functioning within us because we cannot access them on a "thinking" level. They are, for the most part, totally subconscious.

"A belief is a poor substitute for genuine knowledge. A belief is an assumption that is elevated to the status of a conclusion or a truth without an examination and verification through observation and thinking."

—Yasuhiko Genku Kimura, Executive Director of The Twilight Club/Center for Evolutionary Ethics.

I cannot stress enough that these **Reflex/Beliefs** are allowed to operate because we are simply not fully conscious of them. In order to find out which belief is driving us, we must be able to make the correlation between what is going on in our interior lives and the world that buzzes outside of us. Whatever "truth" we see outside of ourselves comes as a direct reaction to what we internally believe about ourselves.

Until we are able to consciously decide which level of energy we wish to manifest, we will not be able to put into place any of the positive changes we desire and deserve. We will keep repeating, over and over, the same familiar, damaging patterns as we continue to blame ourselves and others for anything and everything we perceive as our plight in this life.

Oftentimes, when we suffer emotional distress, our first response is to blame people or situations in our lives. We assume they are the direct cause of our discomfort. It is then that we are making the fatal mistake of reacting to every stressful situation we encounter; this reaction is based on the vast, long-held landscape of negative beliefs that we hold as truths. Some of these are so suppressed we cannot access them.

When we feel angry, hurt, or betrayed, we do and say hurtful and negative things because we feel we are justified in doing so. We have been hurt, and we want whatever the perceived wrong, at the moment it happens, must be immediately corrected. The result this kind of emotion allows is a dangerous continuation of the negative programming that is already in place. In other words, it tells us that all the bad things we think about ourselves are true, which is a lie!

Core negative beliefs surface in early childhood. They are inherited or are born from our perception of ourselves solely based on the way others treat us; they result in all the emotional decisions we make about ourselves. We don't even remember making most of these choices. We suppress and deny them because they are too painful. Carl Jung names this process the "*shadow.*" We all believe we have buried this pain deep within our minds where it will never come to light. But every time we become upset about something, a core negative belief is awakened, and we find ourselves repeating the same old false story. We may have to overcome our "shadow," but we also have access to what Jung termed the "collective unconscious." The "collective unconscious" holds information about the past that we can no longer access. We may claim that we do not believe we are separated from God, but this belief is held in the "collective unconscious." As a result of this, in a way, we are all governed by it. It is like a vast computer system that harbors every pattern created by man for all time. We access it unconsciously, and so, act or react to information without forward, positive thought.

It may seem easier to blame our pain on those we believe caused it, but it is never that which is outside of ourselves that causes our pain. It is only what we have buried deep within ourselves.

In order to make proper use of the Law of Attraction or other Natural and Cosmic Laws, programming contrary to those laws must

4

be resolved. As spiritual leader Melford Okilo tells us in his book *"The Law of Life,"* "Whatever you start doing must inevitably come to an end in you. This is the essence of the Moral Law." As long as a negative belief has a comfortable home in us, it will override any attempt we make to create something different, something better. Let's say we want to generate ten million dollars of financial worth, but our belief system/programming tells us that we deserve to have only ten thousand dollars of financial worth. According to this pattern of logic, we would never be able to manifest the coveted ten million. This is the "Law of Paradoxical Intent" in action, and it works the same way for financial health as it does for any other aspiration, be it love, weight, harmonious relationships, or anything at all.

Following is a list of core negative beliefs. I invite you to make your own list of negative beliefs, so you develop an awareness of the kind of energy with which you are building your world. Until you are fully aware of these negative beliefs, they will keep directing your experiences in life. Once you are conscious of these beliefs, you can build consistent positive thoughts, behaviors, and relationships for yourself.

EXAMPLES OF REFLEX /BELIEFS:

- Abandonment – fear of being left alone
- Failure- fear that you are a fraud and do not deserve success
- Unlovable – fear that you are faulty and will never be loved
- Untrusting – the fear that you are not safe
- Perfectionism - fear that you will never be good enough
- I'm special – the fear that if you are not treated as special, your needs will never be met

These may lead to supporting beliefs such as:

- I have to be strong.

- I don't deserve love.

- I am not appreciated.

- I do not deserve success.

- God is punishing me.

- Nobody cares about me.

- I am not wanted.

- Nobody listens to me.

- Everyone is out to get me.

- I can never get ahead.

LIST YOUR SUPPORTING BELIEFS BELOW:

Chapter 2:
Reactive Thought
Thought Defined

"I am trying to say that thought, it's also the bodily state, the feeling, the nerves. Whatever is going on in the intellectual part connects with everything else."

-David Bohm

"The basic problem with humanity is that the human mind is incapable of discerning truth from falsehood."

-David Hawkins

"Thinking is a dynamic state of motion which conceives patterns, forms and images in a formless universe of space. We create, by thinking patterns or ideas which we call conceptions. We then concentrate our dynamic thought energy into materializing those forms."

-Walter Russell

Thought can be defined as creating new options. We all constantly recycle a lot of information over and over; this makes for repetitive and unoriginal thinking. Like that great old definition of insanity, "doing the exact same thing over and over while expecting different results," this type of cyclical thinking will always give us identical effects.

In his book, *"Wholeness and the Implicate Order,"* David Bohm has this to say about thought: "Thought is, in essence, the active response of memory in every phase of life. We include in thought the intellectual, emotional, sensuous, muscular, and physical responses of memory." This suggests that the thought process is a mechanical one, a repetition of past experience structured from memory. We can then say that there is a great distinction between intelligent thinking and adding intelligence to thought. Ruminating is thought without its core "smarts." It is like a cow chewing her cud, the same thing over and over again. All of us do this sometimes; it is a poorly disguised form of worry. Our ego minds focus on what we do not want to happen, crazily thinking that there is a possibility that we could stop it from happening. Rumination is in no way dynamic or creative; I call it negative prayer. Better thinking, as Bohm says, "…perceive(s) a new order or a new structure that is not just a modification of what is already known or present in memory."

The **THOUGHT** section of the chart is divided into three global categories on each side. The left side of the chart contains the words:

ENLIGHTENMENT: Pure, Sincere, Ineffable, Aware, respectful, appreciating, powerful

Peace: Perfect, Bliss, harmony, trust, thoughtfulness, nurturing, complete

Joy: Serenity, whole, exuberant, fulfilled, energetic, complete, unencumbered

On the right side of the chart are the following words:

APATHY: Waiting to succumb, resigned, hopeless, takes no responsibility for cause, uncared for, insignificant, powerlessness, distrustful, suspicious

SEPARATION/GUILT: Self-destructive, non-entity, "God does not love me. Therefore, I am unlovable," lost, ruined, condemned, ineffectual, conquered.

SHAME: "I won't survive." Humiliation, cowardice, betrayed, dishonored, bad (embarrassed), doubtful.

APATHY

Any belief/reflex or choice we make that manifests itself as separation and takes us away from "Source Energy" is apathy. When we are not willing to hold ourselves accountable for knowing who we are and how we can create our own worlds, apathy reigns. What or whom could we be trying to separate ourselves from? The wholeness of our beings, the "Universal One," "Source Energy," God, in other words, from everyone and everything.

This separation from the sacred is eloquently stated by Andrew Harvey in an article in *New York Naturally* magazine, "Sacred Activism, Facing the Shadow." "Dissociation from the sacred has led to serial holocaust of nature, serial murder of human beings, serial destruction of species… People are in a state of unacknowledged anxiety, dread, suffering, and deep dissociation caused by a fundamental separation from the sacred and from their own deep selves."

Mr. Harvey knows the only way out of this is "…for us to acknowledge the depression and look squarely at what has caused it. This requires each of us to face the reality of what humans have done and continue to do, and turn within to the difficult "shadow work" of realizing those same tendencies in ourselves."

Apathy is the energy that keeps us locked into self-destruction and addiction. To be apathetic means that we have relinquished our power as a divine being. It also allows us to deny responsibility, telling us erroneously that the choices we make are not of our own volition.

On the chart, the reactive *THOUGHT* of Apathy leads to the *Feeling* of Grief and the *Emotion* of Anger/Resentment. Anger/Resentment lets us know we are operating out of a set of beliefs that manifest powerlessness. These beliefs always sound something like this:

"I am no good."

"I am unlovable."

"I am worthless."

"I am uncared for."

"I am a failure."

Our thoughts give power to the beliefs we choose. When this "attractive power" is released into the universal energy field, it attracts the same frequency of energy we send out.

A lot of people may say that apathy is only depression. People say they are depressed, disappointed, and hopeless because they have given up the idea that they can ever have or be what they want. Sometimes, it seems easier to just give up when faced with not getting what we desire. We believe there are no surprises; we know we will not be rewarded. If we do receive what we want, it is just "dumb luck." When we hold this view, in the purest sense, we survive as a victim. There is no personal power or accountability in this scenario.

Laura Lindo of the University of Science and Philosophy calls apathy a "plague" that cripples the world today. Apathy plays out on the world stage as war, poverty, disease, and fear. It is visible daily as people continue to work at jobs they hate and stay in involved relationships that are not fulfilling. There is an incredible high school dropout rate; divorce is on the rise. Our planet and its vital resources are being destroyed and polluted. 2.2 billion Children worldwide live in abject poverty. Children, the elderly, and the disenfranchised are routinely neglected. Species are being serially eradicated. Apathy is having its heyday. It is rampant.

Separation/Guilt are paired because they emanate from a conviction that humanity made a conscious choice long ago to believe that it had removed itself from God and from the reach of His love. The resulting pain we all experience comes from our belief that God is angry with us for leaving him and that He will forever punish each of us for this transgression. This view is a very infantile God's perspective. At best, it is irrational; at worst, it is dangerous because it constantly tells us we have made an unacceptable and irreparable error in taking ourselves away from God. Then comes a whirlwind of fear and self-loathing directed at others in a mad dash to distance ourselves from our perceived wrongdoing. This kind of thinking makes it possible for some to hate and kill others because they believe the "others" are evil, wrong, or just not right with the Lord.

The view, that we are all separate from each other and everything else, is what provokes the destruction of the planet for which we are responsible. The "holding of this belief" is the justification used to decide it is acceptable to destroy rain forests, pollute the waters, over till and pollute the soil, and pollute the air. At a time when it is crucial for our very survival, we must understand we are connected, "One." It is Separation/Guilt that threatens our lives.

Separation/Guilt is a major factor in the destruction of intimate relationships because it perpetuates the mentality that it is always either you or me coming out on top. Relationships become war zones predicated on who will win and who will lose. What we usually fail to realize is if one person in the relationship loses, everyone in the relationship loses.

The **Guilt** aspect of **Separation/Guilt** registers on Dr. David Hawkins' "Map of Consciousness (Power Vs. Force)" at log 30. It reflects a vindictive god-view, blame. The thought is that life is inherently evil, resulting in the leading of a destructive life. Guilt is like the La Brea Tar Pits; it just sucks you under and immobilizes you. Guilt tries to tell you that you have done something terrible and that you need to be punished for it. At times we take the acceptance of our guild to mean that we are manning up and taking responsibility for our bad actions when guilt can never really lead to any positive accountability.

Shame, the last and third level of *Thought* on the chart, holds that position because it is the least acceptable thought option available to us. It is the most painful because it reinforces beliefs that we are evil. It questions our innate goodness as beings. When this untrue belief is triggered, it physically causes us to turn hot and red because it has accessed our most primal sense of survival. We try to deny this concept because we believe we can do nothing to change it.

We think that if others see what we think is "the truth" about ourselves, they will surely reject us immediately. This mistaken view of self creates emotional humiliation. It can, if allowed, wield a power that can result in suicide, homicide, genocide, and nearly every form of abuse.

The vibration of shame cannot support life in any form. It rapidly destroys everything positive. It is the foundation for addictions, which are a false way to safety from shame's nagging.

I placed **Shame** at this position on the chart because Apathy and Separation/Guilt are the only means of avoiding looking Shame in the face. We fear Shame will literally kill us if we come face to face with it. Apathy and Separation/Guilt can function as protective devices until we find the courage within ourselves to face the "dragon" of Shame.

Chapter 3:
Thought Level: Pro-Active State Of Mind
[Left side of the *EMCS Living In Choice© Chart*]

The **Pro-Active State of Mind** side of the chart comes from the truth of who we are; we are spiritual beings having a productive human experience. It represents our birthright. This is not a state of mind we have to earn; it has always existed and is available at any moment that we choose to access it. We do, however, have to choose it.

Survival messages coming from **Separation/Guilt** cause us to repeat habitual survival behaviors, blocking out the better voice within. Learning to listen to this voice and act upon what it tells you will allow you to live the loving and harmonious life that we all desire.

ENLIGHTENMENT: pure, sincere, ineffable

The life we desire is only available through a **PROACTIVE** rather than a **REACTIVE** state of mind. The proactive Thought side of the chart starts with **Enlightenment: Pure, Sincere, and Ineffable.** A conscious connection with your Higher Self is pure. Sin need never enter into this. Sin is archery jargon; it simply means to miss the mark. Some say the word "sincere" comes from *sem*, meaning "one," and *cerus*, a derivative of the Latin word *crescere,* which means "to grow." It can be said that to be sincere means to grow into "the one" to become one with "the one."

PEACE: perfect, blissful

The second Thought level on the **Pro-Active State of Mind** side of the chart is peopled with the likes of Mother Teresa, Martin Luther King, Peace Pilgrim, Walter Russell, Nelson Mandela, and His Holiness, the Dali Lama. It is a level of consciousness we all dream of. It comes in a moment of Divine Inspiration where all mental activity stops. A sense of timelessness comes over one, and inspiration flows in the way rain refreshes a hot summer afternoon. A renewed sense of enthusiasm, calm, and joy fills the person. Everything is joyfully connected to everything else.

JOY: complete, serenity

The third Thought level, **Joy,** is a desire to use our own consciousness for the illumination and benefit of life itself rather than one's own selfish gain. This creates a capacity to love many people simultaneously. Obviously, the more one loves, the more one can continue to love.

Joy comes to us as freedom in the physical body. Our physical selves reflect an exuberant participation in all aspects of life. Joy shows in one's face, step, and voice. Joy is unmistakably contagious to all with whom we come in contact. Living each moment in joy will bring us all long, healthy, and prosperous lives. From joy comes the ability to love music, art, and the laughter of a child. Inner harmony and serenity always come from absorbing joy.

Chapter 4:
Reactive Feelings Level

EXPLANATION

The middle level of the *EMCS Living In Choice© Chart,* the *Feeling* level, reflects the energy we give power to the thoughts on which we choose to focus. Three global levels of feeling result:

Thought: APATHY creates the *Feeling*, which is GRIEF.

Separation/Guilt creates the *Feeling*: FEAR.

SHAME creates the *Feeling*: Desire/Hostility.

Feelings do not stand alone. They operate on the information that comes from giving energy and focus to any particular thought. Feelings give us information about what we are instantly creating in our own personal energy system. Feelings are never right or wrong, good or bad. They give us two types of information - our needs are being met, or our needs are not being met.

This awareness gives rise to the question, "If my needs are not being met, what is my next step." Or "My needs are being me, I want more of this!"

It is necessary to build a vocabulary of our feelings in order to be radically personally responsible for our own inner words. Being aware of what our bodies tell us they feel gives us a map to see where the information we digest is coming from. Is it coming only from our survival mode? Is it triggered by a past negative experience? If these questions ring the least bit true, we now have opportunities to clear out many misconceptions that we hold about ourselves.

Sometimes, a feeling gives us information about something outside ourselves. Perhaps another person is projecting his or her own shame, guilt, or anger onto us. This is not about us. We can always be present in the situation without taking it on as our own. Compassion for others who are in pain is never a negative thing. Remember, we are not always appropriately aware of what is going on inside of ourselves. Sometimes, we are too close to someone or a situation, or we are in too much pain ourselves. A great thing to say might go something like this, "I see how disappointed you are that the situation didn't work out the way you wanted it to." Your observation mirrors the other person's pain. You are honoring their sadness and caring enough to be there with them as they pass through it, but you are also gently letting them know that you cannot fix it.

Identified feelings feed us facts about what we need in specific situations. When we Identify our own needs, we put ourselves high on the road to loving ourselves. This makes us able to hold ourselves accountable for our own personal belief system. It will birth courage in us that will aid us in getting our needs met in appropriate ways.

Anger lets us know, loud and clear, that our needs are not being met. If we believe that someone else is responsible for meeting our needs and they, in our eyes, fail to get the job done, then one of our core negative beliefs will be triggered. This negative belief may try to tell us that we are not important. Ideas like this kick-start APATHY, GRIEF, and ANGER/RESENTMENT. Now, the fight is on, and we endlessly blame other people for not loving and respecting us. This is a self-defeating survival pattern that results in a never-ending power struggle. It separates us not only from ourselves but from everyone else as well.

GRIEF: regret, despondent, tragic, self-blame, victim

Stemming from APATHY comes the feeling of GRIEF with Its attendants: regret, despondent, tragic, self-blame, and victim energies. Dr. David Hawkins says, "…Grief is the cemetery of life." It is a level of sadness and brokenheartedness that is tragic because it instructs us to give up our own power. It tells us, mistakenly, that we can never replace what we think we have lost. It engenders self-blame to the point that we become victims of our own wrong-mindedness. Grief colors our vision of life and causes depression. For instance, if we follow this path, the loss of a loved one may come to mean the loss of love itself.

FEAR: anxiety, avoidance, escape, "Something will be taken away from me."

FEAR stems from a SEPARATION/GUILT thought, which tells us we have done something wrong and need to be punished for it. Thus, we fear the punishment that should surely now come. The question of when it will come is elusive and ever-present. Dr. Hawkins says that "…once fear is one's focus, the endless fearful events of the world feed it. Fear becomes obsessive and may take any form; fear of loss of a relationship leads to jealousy and a chronically high-stress level. Fearful thinking can balloon into paranoia or generate neurotic defensive structures and, because it is contagious, become a dominant social trend."

The *Thought* of SHAME stokes the fire of the feeling DESIRE/HOSTILITY and creates the need to project it onto someone else. Just blame others: Someone else is responsible for me not getting what I want. This is the energy of desperation and greed. It can move us to expend a lot of energy to achieve a goal only to leave us feeling let down as reaching the goal did not fill our bottomless pit of desire. We start to feel hostile because we can't fulfill our endless needs. This is the level of addiction "...wherein desire becomes a craving more important than life itself," says Hawkins.

Chapter 5:
Pro-Active Feelings Side

LOVE: reverent, benign, revelatory

The Proactive State of Mind thoughts of **ENLIGHTENMENT, PEACE, and JOY** generate Pro-Active feeling states of **LOVE, REASON, and ACCEPTANCE** and emotions of **NEUTRAL, WILLING, AND COURAGE.** We will take them in order:

The feeling of **LOVE** I refer to here is the expression/result one would expect from the Thoughtsource: **pure, sincere, ineffable enlightenment**. It is the energy of "Light" given freely without conditions or limits. Because of its unconditional and limitless origin, this source of love expresses a gentle, kind, and gracious revelation and celebration. Dr. Hawkins says of his Energy Level of Love: "Love takes no position and thus is global, rising above the separation of positionality. It is then possible to be 'one with another.'" This expression of love honors and includes all and expands itself simultaneously. True happiness stems from this expression of the **Thought of Enlightenment** and the **Feeling of Love**.

Lazarus, who channels through Jack Pursel, says of love, "We love another so that we may grow." This statement can only be true for us if we have the awareness stemming from a proactive state of mind. Love lets us see the bigger picture. It helps us escape our ego-driven mind and frees us from what Colin Tipping, author of "Radical Forgiveness," calls "Victim-land."

REASON: wise, understanding

The **PRO-ACTIVE: State of Mind** - *Thought* of **Peace: perfect, blissful** stimulates the *FEELING* of **REASON: wise and understanding**. Only in a state of mind in which we are peacefully aware of our surroundings and ourselves can we begin to explore science, education, and the advancement of knowledge. **REASON**, being a purely intellectual pursuit, can miss life's nuances when sought for its own sake. Internalization of the information that **REASON** seeks from us then shoves wisdom into action. It takes the form of **understanding**. Then, it is able to transform mere intellectual pursuits into service. The first service is to the One Law or the Universal One, the second is to the self, and the third is to others. What greater service can there be?

ACCEPTANCE: harmonious, forgiving

The *Thought* **JOY** causes the *Feeling* of **ACCEPTANCE,** giving rise to **COURAGE,** providing the harmonious expression of life that is fully capable of forgiveness. **ACCEPTANCE** lets us know that everything in this life happens for a reason. Every incident is full of purpose; there are no coincidences, ever. "Stuff" does not just happen. Nothing in life is a random event. Hawkins says, "With **acceptance,** there is emotional calm, and perception is widened as denial is transcended. One now sees things without distortion or misinterpretation; the context of experience is expanded so that one is capable of 'seeing the whole picture.'"

For the sake of clarity, feelings are the result of the interpretation of internal and external impressions and sensations identified by the awareness function of the mind, which includes the five senses. The awareness function is our guidance system. Internally, the awareness function translates impressions and sensations into feelings. When your feelings signal information such as fear, anger, distress, or unhappiness, it is the "job" of the Observer "I," which is also a component of the awareness function, to investigate the factuality of the information. If the information is not true, does it stem from a triggered core negative belief? Discerning the truth about the information that the feelings represent leads the Observer "I" to report the lie and, thus, change the response to the information from reaction to pro-action. It is correct to say that feelings are not right or wrong, not good or bad. Feelings are just information we use along life's journey. Once wisdom, attuned and aware, becomes our state of being, we learn to listen to this guidance. Fear and denial no longer have a place in our lives. Waking the Observer "I" makes it possible for guidance from the Universal One to move us toward life's fulfillment.

Chapter 6:
Reactive Emotional

ANGER/RESENTMENT

EMOTION is energy in motion or E-motion, and is the result of giving constant energy to a *Belief/Reflex*: **THOUGHT, or FEELING,** which expresses that energy into the outer world. This is the strongest energy we emit. It is received by the Law of Attraction and mirrored to us in form. This is the final step in co-creating our world. I say co-create because there must be some Intelligence or Creative Mind that participates. The Law of Attraction exhibits the qualities inherent in all universal laws by consistently acting the same way; it is always present and always neutral. The Law of Attraction mirrors to us what we project onto it with exactly the same energy with which we release the emotion, the way a physical mirror reflects the light of a candle set before it. It never reflects more or less light, only the precise amount present in the candle.

This neutral, loving law operates at all times, whether we are aware of it or not. Awareness of the law, how it operates, and our relationship with it become essential to the co-creation of our outer world. We understand that we create our world through the expression of our beliefs, thoughts, feelings, and emotions.

The final level of the chart, *Emotion*, begins with **ANGER/RESENTMENT**. These are paired because when we have given up our power and succumbed to Apathy, we delve into Grief. We do this because we feel we have no power in and of ourselves to meet our own needs. In **GRIEF**, our 'victim' either internalizes the blame or projects it onto someone else or situation. **ANGER** stems from the **RESENTMENT** for not getting the expected results. **ANGER/RESENTMENT** becomes something to hide behind as if we are saying, "You hurt me, and that gives me the right to protect myself." This is evidence of an expectation that it is someone else's responsibility to meet our needs. Now, that person(s) or situation is being blamed for harming us. This whole scenario is evidence of a system that sets up an individual who is in grief as a "victim," and the offending person(s) or situation is seen as the perpetrator. This expunges any personal accountability. In other words, "It has to be someone else's fault, or I would not feel so angry."

As unproductive as this system is, it seems to be the default projection in the world today. We commonly hear reporters asking the question, "Didn't that make you angry?" This implies that the person being questioned is the victim of some wrongdoing. Handy as it is to absolve oneself of accountability, it does absolutely nothing to resolve issues and create world peace.

PRIDE/INDIFFERENCE

False **PRIDE** is married to **INDIFFERENCE** because false pride acts as if it has no feelings about an external experience that is actually the cause of internal pain. This is a survival mechanism that covers **FEAR** and **APATHY**. When the fear of loss and feeling of hopelessness hover just beneath the surface, ready to explode in bouts of desperation, false **PRIDE** is the bravado that says, "I can handle it." or "I don't care." As Dr. David Hawkins says, "Pride goeth before a fall…Pride is defensive and vulnerable to attack. Pride remains weak because it can be knocked off its pedestal into Shame, which is the threat that fires the fear of loss of pride." In addition, he says that "…the whole problem of denial is pride." It is easy to see pride used as an emotional, political tool when listening to the current ongoing debate about bringing our troops home from Iraq. The whole issue concerning support or not support of our troops in Iraq is one of pride. It throws us off the track of denial that it covers. There are always two sides to a story. When one side is condemned as less than the other side, pride and denial are both coloring the story. It is pride that keeps countries at war and families separated, fighting, and polarized over a particular point of view.

ANTAGONISM

ANTAGONISM is the cover-up for **inadequacy.** It is supported by the feeling of **Desire/Hostility** and the thought of **SHAME**, which is attended by humiliation. The language of **SHAME** is "I won't survive." **ANTAGONISM** is another form of projection and denial. The antagonist's goal is to redirect attention from himself/herself onto someone or something else. **ANTAGONISM** is hostile and destructive and twists the truth in order to suit its own agenda. It is reactive and unreasonable. It is destructive to itself, others, and the environment because the underlying negative belief says annihilation is close at hand. **ANTAGONISM** seems a better bargain than ever-present **SHAME.**

Chapter 7:
Pro-Active Emotional Side

NEUTRAL: trust, satisfied . . .

The car is running; the driver is in the seat, ready to

choose a gear and direction. The mirrors are set;

the brake is released, all systems are ready to go.

The driver is alert, secure in her ability to drive the

car and move in any direction at will. She trusts

the car will make the trip. There is a complete

absence of fear, doubt, insecurity. NEUTRAL is

supported by the FEELING of LOVE and the

THOUGHT of ENLIGHTENMENT.

Dr. Hawkins describes his consciousness level of Neutral in this manner, "...to be relatively unattached to outcomes...not getting one's way is no longer experienced as defeating, frightening or frustrating." The emotional level of neutral is characterized by a sense of peace and fulfillment that is not interested in guilt, conflict, or competition. There are no hidden agendas.

WILLING: intentional, optimistic . . .

WILLING is the emotional expression arising from the *Feeling* of **Reason (wise, understanding)** and the *Thought* of **PEACE: perfect, blissful**. Inherent in **WILLING** is the power to move toward an intention with optimism. It holds, within it, resources to take action and fulfill the mission. The wisdom and understanding that has come from an experience is the foundation upon which a new situation or relationship can be built.

In Dr. Hawkins' Map Of Consciousness, willingness is a level of "high self-esteem," which is mirrored by society in the form of acknowledgement and recognition. Willingness moves us to a place of **COURAGE**, the next level on the *EMCS Living in Choice Levels of Responsibility Chart*.

COURAGE: affirming, empowered, feasible. . .

COURAGE sees life through an affirming view and empowers the feasibility of achieving any aim we set for ourselves. **Joy** and **Acceptance** support bravery through **COURAGE** making life fun, exciting, and fulfilling. People who operate out of **Courage** are able to set forth just as much energy into the world as they take out of it. **COURAGE** faces fears and self-doubts and moves through those fears and self-doubts into the light of day. Like the Cowardly Lion in the movie "The Wizard of Oz," **COURAGE** allows us to find the heart through which we live a life of compassion and understanding. Without **COURAGE,** we are delegated to a life of suffering, pain, and sorrow. **COURAGE** enables us to accomplish anything.

Chapter 8:
Final Words

The **REACTIVE** side of the **EMCS Living In Choice Levels of Responsibility Chart** is called the "river of denial" because it is insidious, seductive, and automatic. It baffles us that we can live our lives in this river while knowing, on some level, that it never makes us happy nor fulfills us. It does nothing to enhance personal, business, or family relationships. It drags us down into a pit of despair, yet we keep on swimming.

The **PRO-ACTIVE** side of the chart is the aim we have been seeking. Most of us have been searching outside ourselves only to discover that it is not "out there." It is within us.

It is my prayer that you will find this chart helpful in searching the internal world of cause.

THE LIVING IN CHOICE SCIENCE OF MANIFESTATION

The Next Step on the Journey

I don't know about you, but I spent most of my life pushing, struggling, and fighting to get somewhere other than where I was at the time. Perhaps it was the old saying, "The grass is always greener on the other side," that kept me seeking, or maybe it was something innate that was and continues to be the driver. At any rate, somewhere along the way, I decided to stop the struggle and spend time learning how this thing we call life works.

My intention was and is to awaken to the reality that we create our reality through energy in all its expressions: generating, expressing, and manifesting. I just wanted to spend my time utilizing the energies within and without to support my health, wealth, and joy. I was sick to death of the shotgun effect and wanted to be laser-like and efficient in co-creating my moments. Truthfully, I was looking for some magic bullet, some "secret," to instantaneously make me rich, famous, and powerful. My thought was that happiness would come along with those manifestations. When I paused and examined the lives of the rich, famous, and powerful, I discovered that happiness did not necessarily follow those manifestations. This leads me to jump headlong into the study of works of masters that have survived the ravages of time and human tampering. In the sometimes tattered pages of a dusty old tome, I began to wake up to a Universal Truth: Everything is energy. Energy can change form, but it does not die.

This awareness caused me to think of myself as an energy form - a dynamic, pulsating, ever-changing field of energy. It was mind-boggling to think about myself and other human beings as fields of energy with a driver we call consciousness. It also became clear to me that there are many levels of consciousness; it seems each level manifests in different life experiences. Dr. David Hawkins explains this in his mind-blowing book *Power Vs Force*. This clarity of understanding led me to ponder, "How can I utilize my own energy field and consciousness to achieve the results I desire in my own life?"

Dr. David Bohm, the renowned physicist who worked with Albert Einstein during the last six months of Einstein's life, inspired me, in his book, *Thought As A System*, to focus my attention on the process of thought itself. This study eventually led me to create the chart I call The Science of Manifestation©. I have used this, with my clients in my private practice, as a learning tool for many years and have found that it helps my clients identify the correlation between what they believe, think, feel, and emote and their life experience(s). This process is a form of self-accountability in which they can clearly see the outcome without having to live out the belief, should they choose to carry the belief to completion.

Once I understood the connection between belief and its resultant manipulation of energy or manifestation of a life expression, filling in the blanks became easy. Identifying a belief is not so simple. I like the definition of belief Kimura shares in his book *The Twilight Manifesto*; "A belief is a poor substitute for genuine knowledge. A belief is an assumption that is elevated to the status of a conclusion or truth without examination and verification through observation and thinking. There are only two basic epistemological possibilities: that is, either you know or you don't know. A belief is the violation of epistemological integrity in which something one doesn't really know is feigned as something one knows. Therefore, the act of believing is a form of intellectual self-deception and ineluctably leads to the suppression of questioning or doubting, which in turn leads to the phenomenon of "true-believers" or "fundamentalists" - fanaticism and arrogance that are caused by a morbid fear of one's own suppressed doubt and by insecurity."

It is easy, using this definition, to see that the cause of the condition of the world today lies in this misperception of reality. Attempting to make something other than what it is is crazy-making, and the energy it takes to convince, manipulate, control, prejudice, hate, and annihilate that which says otherwise is destructive and debilitating. Perhaps you have been aware of this pattern operating in your own world. Have you ever tried to convince yourself that something was one way when, in reality, it was not that way at all? Think of the time, energy, and constant mind chatter it took to keep that false story alive. It is just mind-boggling, isn't it?

The Living in Choice Science of Manifestation Chart© is a simple form designed to help you identify the various forms of energy, thought, feeling, and emotion that ultimately manifest your life experience. Manifesting that which one desires is a process and system of identifying an idea (Thought), giving it energy (Feeling), expressing it through Emotion (energy in motion), giving it voice (language), and taking a physical action (Action) toward that which you desire to manifest (Manifestation). Most people are not aware that what they think, feel, emote, say, and act upon results in physical manifestations.

It is important to understand that unconscious beliefs can interfere with a conscious desire to create or manifest an idea into form. If a core negative belief states, "It is sinful to be rich," then gaining wealth will be sabotaged no matter what you do. Even if you do gain a modicum of wealth, it will be whittled away by seemingly unrelated events: illness, accidents, unprofitable investments, conmen, or the like. You may find yourself saying things like, "No matter what I do, I don't seem to be able to stay ahead of the game."

I cannot stress enough the importance of ferreting out the pesky negative beliefs that lay hidden in the subconscious and unconscious mind. These beliefs were stored up in childhood and inherited from parents, grandparents, and, perhaps, even past life karma. Taking the time to complete and examine your Science of Manifestation Chart enables you to discover your beliefs or, at least, find a clue to your underlying negative beliefs. You can use the list of core negative beliefs in the text to assist you in identifying yours.

Let's look at an example. You realize you are feeling angry or resentful about some life experience and want to blame external circumstances rather than taking responsibility for the internal cause. After second thought, you decide to look within to see what core negative belief is operative in this situation. Utilizing the steps identified by the Living in Choice Levels of Responsibility Chart© (on the following page) to assist, you begin to plug in the known components in red.

The Four Steps in The Science of Manifestation©

1. BECOME AWARE OF THE NEGATIVE PATTERN.

2. IDENTIFY THE THOUGHT, FEELING, EMOTION, LANGUAGE, ETC.

3. INTERVENE BY QUESTIONING THE THOUGHT, USING: WHO, WHAT, WHERE; NEVER WHY or HOW! Ask yourself: What is true here? Will this thought produce the outcome I desire?

4. CREATE A NEW FOCUS OR A NEW THOUGHT AND FOLLOW IT THROUGH THE STEPS OF BELIEF, THOUGHT, FEELING, EMOTION, LANGUAGE, ACTION, AND MANIFESTATION.

Living In Choice Science of Manifestation Chart©

Belief	Thought	Feeling	Emotion	Language	Action	Manifestation
I'm not valuable	Apathy	Grief	Anger/ Resentment	Blaming	Destructive	Separation
Maybe, I'm Valuable	Peaceful	Reason	Willing	I can language	Life-enhancing action	Unity

Let's break this down.

- The anger/resentment was easy to spot on the Levels of Responsibility Chart as an emotional response. Plug that in the emotion column on the chart. Once you have identified a thought, feeling, or emotion, the rest is easy. Look at the Levels of Responsibility Chart and identify the thought based on the already identified emotion. Remember, the Levels of Responsibility Chart is set up in such a way that, for instance, apathy generates grief, which in turn generates the emotion of anger/resentment.
- Under "Language," write down the language that has been running around in your head or coming out of your mouth. Determine the quality of that language: destructive, self-sabotaging, judgmental language; peaceful, calm, and life-affirming. Enter this in the language column.
- Move to the ACTION column. Determine the physical action you normally employ to generate the outcome (MANIFESTATION).
- Move to MANIFESTATION. This column gives you the opportunity to determine what will be the outcome of putting into action the thought, feeling, emotion, language, and action. Before acting on it see on paper what the results will be. Determine for yourself if you desire the consequences or manifestation that is inevitable if you put it into action.

Since this is a system, the thought, feeling, emotion, language, action, and manifestation must originate from some source. That source is the belief that triggered the reaction. The end result is only a reflection of the belief. Taking a clue from apathy, which indicates a giving up of one's power, seeing oneself as hopeless, helpless, and a non-entity, it seems reasonable that the belief/reflex might be "I have no value" or "I am not important" in this particular situation. Thus stimulating the reaction that follows.

- Once determined what is really going on, the next step in the sequence is to determine the truth or reality rather than, once again, operating from the same old "story" of your victimhood.

- Once you have completed the above, you have accomplished steps 1 and 2 of the Living in Choice Science of Manifestation Chart©. Step three is the intervention. Wake up the observer "I" by questioning the belief or the thought. Some good questions are: "What does this mean about for me if I put this into action?", "Where will this take me?" "Do I really want to play this out?" "What is the truth here?"

Asking and answering these questions leads to new thoughts, allowing for a PRO-ACTIVE response to the situation. Once you are certain that you do not want to go down the old path, again, go to step 4.

- Utilizing your Living in Choice Responsibility Chart, look at the left side of the chart as you are facing it and determine a better response in the form of belief, thought, feeling, emotion, language, action, and manifestation. For an example look back at the chart above in the second row in green lettering. Remember, this is a powerful system driven by the universal energy of creation. The choice to see yourself as valuable generates Peace (perfect, blissful), Reason (wise, understanding), and Willing (intentional, optimistic), leading to "I can" language and life-enhancing action, which results in attracting people and resources that you need for success. You can find unity within yourself and with others. Isn't that what we are all looking for?

This process can be enhanced by utilizing The Cone Center For Living In Choice© Worksheet available at www.garycone.com

CREDENTIALS

Dr. Cone's doctorate is in Energy Medicine. He holds a Diplomate in Comprehensive Energy Psychology, a State of Oklahoma Licensed Alcohol, Drug, and Mental Health Counselor, a Master Addiction Counselor, a Reiki Master, and a Certified Master Radical Living Practitioner. Dr. Cone offices in Oklahoma City and does long-distance sessions. You may purchase a session from his website, www.garycone.com, or call 405-842-0695 to schedule an appointment.

Dr. Cone created the Energy Matrix Clearing System©, a form of Energy Psychology/Energy Medicine. This is a comprehensive process utilizing the entire human holographic energy system to effect clearing energy blockages that support ill health in all aspects of the system. Over the last 30 years, Dr. Cone has perfected this system, and the results speak for themselves. He utilizes this system in his Twenty-One Day Addictions process.

For more information, go to www.garycone.com

Dedication

I dedicate this work to the human species with the loving intent that they find here a way to create for themselves a world of peace, love, health, and opulence.

Acknowledgement

This work could not be except for those Great Minds, both ancient and modern, who, with loving hearts and sincere dedication to a path of enlightenment, have left their indelible mark on the energetic matrix of the Unified Field for those "with eyes to see" and "ears to hear."

You have my most humble and heartfelt thanks!

www.ingramcontent.com/pod-product-compliance
Lightning Source LLC
Chambersburg PA
CBHW041308020426
42333CB00001B/14